This notebook belongs to:

_____

Published by: Character Designs

SAVINGS Goal Tracker

Saving for: _____   Amount needed: _____   Due date: _____

DATE	AMOUNT SAVED	SAVINGS BALANCE	STILL NEED TO SAVE....

NOTES

_____

_____

_____

_____

SAVINGS Goal Tracker

Saving for: _____   Amount needed: _____   Due date: _____

DATE	AMOUNT SAVED	SAVINGS BALANCE	STILL NEED TO SAVE....

NOTES

_____

_____

_____

_____

SAVINGS Goal Tracker

Saving for: _____   Amount needed: _____   Due date: _____

DATE	AMOUNT SAVED	SAVINGS BALANCE	STILL NEED TO SAVE....

NOTES

_____

_____

_____

_____

_____

SAVINGS Goal Tracker

Saving for: _____   Amount needed: _____   Due date: _____

DATE	AMOUNT SAVED	SAVINGS BALANCE	STILL NEED TO SAVE....

NOTES

_____

_____

_____

_____

SAVINGS Goal Tracker

Saving for: _____   Amount needed: _____   Due date: _____

DATE	AMOUNT SAVED	SAVINGS BALANCE	STILL NEED TO SAVE....

NOTES

_____

_____

_____

_____

SAVINGS Goal Tracker

Saving for: _____   Amount needed: _____   Due date: _____

DATE	AMOUNT SAVED	SAVINGS BALANCE	STILL NEED TO SAVE....

NOTES

_____

_____

_____

_____

SAVINGS Goal Tracker

Saving for: _____   Amount needed:_____   Due date:_____

DATE	AMOUNT SAVED	SAVINGS BALANCE	STILL NEED TO SAVE....

NOTES

_____
_____
_____
_____

SAVINGS Goal Tracker

Saving for: _____   Amount needed: _____   Due date: _____

DATE	AMOUNT SAVED	SAVINGS BALANCE	STILL NEED TO SAVE....

NOTES

_____

_____

_____

_____

SAVINGS Goal Tracker

Saving for: _____   Amount needed: _____   Due date: _____

DATE	AMOUNT SAVED	SAVINGS BALANCE	STILL NEED TO SAVE....

NOTES

_____

_____

_____

_____

SAVINGS Goal Tracker

Saving for: _____   Amount needed: _____   Due date: _____

DATE	AMOUNT SAVED	SAVINGS BALANCE	STILL NEED TO SAVE....

NOTES

_____

_____

_____

_____

SAVINGS Goal Tracker

Saving for: _____   Amount needed: _____   Due date: _____

DATE	AMOUNT SAVED	SAVINGS BALANCE	STILL NEED TO SAVE....

NOTES

_____

_____

_____

_____

_____

SAVINGS Goal Tracker

Saving for: _____   Amount needed: _____   Due date: _____

DATE	AMOUNT SAVED	SAVINGS BALANCE	STILL NEED TO SAVE....

NOTES

_____

_____

_____

_____

_____

SAVINGS Goal Tracker

Saving for: _____   Amount needed: _____   Due date: _____

DATE	AMOUNT SAVED	SAVINGS BALANCE	STILL NEED TO SAVE....

NOTES

_____

_____

_____

_____

SAVINGS Goal Tracker

Saving for: _____   Amount needed: _____   Due date: _____

DATE	AMOUNT SAVED	SAVINGS BALANCE	STILL NEED TO SAVE....

NOTES

_____

_____

_____

_____

SAVINGS Goal Tracker

Saving for: _____   Amount needed: _____   Due date: _____

DATE	AMOUNT SAVED	SAVINGS BALANCE	STILL NEED TO SAVE....

NOTES

_____

_____

_____

_____

SAVINGS Goal Tracker

Saving for: _____   Amount needed: _____   Due date: _____

DATE	AMOUNT SAVED	SAVINGS BALANCE	STILL NEED TO SAVE....

NOTES

_____
_____
_____
_____

SAVINGS Goal Tracker

Saving for: _____   Amount needed: _____   Due date: _____

DATE	AMOUNT SAVED	SAVINGS BALANCE	STILL NEED TO SAVE....

NOTES

_____

_____

_____

_____

SAVINGS Goal Tracker

Saving for: _____   Amount needed: _____   Due date: _____

DATE	AMOUNT SAVED	SAVINGS BALANCE	STILL NEED TO SAVE....

NOTES

_____

_____

_____

_____

SAVINGS Goal Tracker

Saving for: _____   Amount needed: _____   Due date: _____

DATE	AMOUNT SAVED	SAVINGS BALANCE	STILL NEED TO SAVE....

NOTES

_____

_____

_____

_____

SAVINGS Goal Tracker

Saving for: _____   Amount needed: _____   Due date: _____

DATE	AMOUNT SAVED	SAVINGS BALANCE	STILL NEED TO SAVE….

NOTES

_____

_____

_____

_____

SAVINGS Goal Tracker

Saving for: _____   Amount needed: _____   Due date: _____

DATE	AMOUNT SAVED	SAVINGS BALANCE	STILL NEED TO SAVE....

NOTES

_____

_____

_____

_____

SAVINGS Goal Tracker

Saving for: _____   Amount needed: _____   Due date: _____

DATE	AMOUNT SAVED	SAVINGS BALANCE	STILL NEED TO SAVE....

NOTES

_____

_____

_____

_____

SAVINGS Goal Tracker

Saving for: _____   Amount needed: _____   Due date: _____

DATE	AMOUNT SAVED	SAVINGS BALANCE	STILL NEED TO SAVE....

NOTES

_____

_____

_____

_____

SAVINGS Goal Tracker

Saving for: _____   Amount needed: _____   Due date: _____

DATE	AMOUNT SAVED	SAVINGS BALANCE	STILL NEED TO SAVE....

NOTES

_____

_____

_____

_____

SAVINGS Goal Tracker

Saving for: _____   Amount needed: _____   Due date: _____

DATE	AMOUNT SAVED	SAVINGS BALANCE	STILL NEED TO SAVE....

NOTES

_____

_____

_____

_____

SAVINGS Goal Tracker

Saving for: _____   Amount needed: _____   Due date: _____

DATE	AMOUNT SAVED	SAVINGS BALANCE	STILL NEED TO SAVE....

NOTES

_____

_____

_____

_____

SAVINGS Goal Tracker

Saving for: _____   Amount needed: _____   Due date: _____

DATE	AMOUNT SAVED	SAVINGS BALANCE	STILL NEED TO SAVE....

NOTES

_____

_____

_____

_____

SAVINGS Goal Tracker

Saving for: _____   Amount needed: _____   Due date: _____

DATE	AMOUNT SAVED	SAVINGS BALANCE	STILL NEED TO SAVE....

NOTES

_____

_____

_____

_____

SAVINGS Goal Tracker

Saving for: _____   Amount needed:_____   Due date:_____

DATE	AMOUNT SAVED	SAVINGS BALANCE	STILL NEED TO SAVE....

NOTES

_____

_____

_____

_____

SAVINGS Goal Tracker

Saving for: _____   Amount needed: _____   Due date: _____

DATE	AMOUNT SAVED	SAVINGS BALANCE	STILL NEED TO SAVE....

NOTES

_____

_____

_____

_____

SAVINGS Goal Tracker

Saving for: _____   Amount needed: _____   Due date: _____

DATE	AMOUNT SAVED	SAVINGS BALANCE	STILL NEED TO SAVE....

NOTES

_____

_____

_____

_____

SAVINGS Goal Tracker

Saving for: _____   Amount needed: _____   Due date: _____

DATE	AMOUNT SAVED	SAVINGS BALANCE	STILL NEED TO SAVE....

NOTES

_____

_____

_____

_____

SAVINGS Goal Tracker

Saving for: _____   Amount needed: _____   Due date: _____

DATE	AMOUNT SAVED	SAVINGS BALANCE	STILL NEED TO SAVE....

NOTES

_____

_____

_____

_____

SAVINGS Goal Tracker

Saving for: _____   Amount needed: _____   Due date: _____

DATE	AMOUNT SAVED	SAVINGS BALANCE	STILL NEED TO SAVE....

NOTES

_____

_____

_____

_____

SAVINGS Goal Tracker

Saving for: _____   Amount needed: _____   Due date: _____

DATE	AMOUNT SAVED	SAVINGS BALANCE	STILL NEED TO SAVE....

NOTES

_____

_____

_____

_____

SAVINGS Goal Tracker

Saving for: _____   Amount needed: _____   Due date: _____

DATE	AMOUNT SAVED	SAVINGS BALANCE	STILL NEED TO SAVE....

NOTES

_____

_____

_____

_____

SAVINGS Goal Tracker

Saving for: _____   Amount needed: _____   Due date: _____

DATE	AMOUNT SAVED	SAVINGS BALANCE	STILL NEED TO SAVE....

NOTES

_____

_____

_____

_____

SAVINGS Goal Tracker

Saving for: _____   Amount needed:_____   Due date:_____

DATE	AMOUNT SAVED	SAVINGS BALANCE	STILL NEED TO SAVE....

NOTES

_____

_____

_____

_____

SAVINGS Goal Tracker

Saving for: _____   Amount needed: _____   Due date: _____

DATE	AMOUNT SAVED	SAVINGS BALANCE	STILL NEED TO SAVE....

NOTES

_____
_____
_____
_____

SAVINGS Goal Tracker

Saving for: _____   Amount needed: _____   Due date: _____

DATE	AMOUNT SAVED	SAVINGS BALANCE	STILL NEED TO SAVE....

NOTES

_____

_____

_____

_____

SAVINGS Goal Tracker

Saving for: _____   Amount needed: _____   Due date: _____

DATE	AMOUNT SAVED	SAVINGS BALANCE	STILL NEED TO SAVE....

NOTES

_____

_____

_____

_____

SAVINGS Goal Tracker

Saving for: _____ Amount needed: _____ Due date: _____

DATE	AMOUNT SAVED	SAVINGS BALANCE	STILL NEED TO SAVE....

NOTES

_____

_____

_____

_____

SAVINGS Goal Tracker

Saving for: _____   Amount needed: _____   Due date: _____

DATE	AMOUNT SAVED	SAVINGS BALANCE	STILL NEED TO SAVE....

NOTES

_____

_____

_____

_____

SAVINGS Goal Tracker

Saving for: _____   Amount needed: _____   Due date: _____

DATE	AMOUNT SAVED	SAVINGS BALANCE	STILL NEED TO SAVE....

NOTES

_____

_____

_____

_____

SAVINGS Goal Tracker

Saving for: _____   Amount needed: _____   Due date: _____

DATE	AMOUNT SAVED	SAVINGS BALANCE	STILL NEED TO SAVE....

NOTES

_____

_____

_____

_____

SAVINGS Goal Tracker

Saving for: _____   Amount needed: _____   Due date: _____

DATE	AMOUNT SAVED	SAVINGS BALANCE	STILL NEED TO SAVE....

NOTES

_____

_____

_____

_____

SAVINGS Goal Tracker

Saving for: _____   Amount needed: _____   Due date: _____

DATE	AMOUNT SAVED	SAVINGS BALANCE	STILL NEED TO SAVE....

NOTES

_____

_____

_____

_____

SAVINGS Goal Tracker

Saving for: _____   Amount needed: _____   Due date: _____

DATE	AMOUNT SAVED	SAVINGS BALANCE	STILL NEED TO SAVE....

NOTES

_____

_____

_____

_____

SAVINGS Goal Tracker

Saving for: _____   Amount needed: _____   Due date: _____

DATE	AMOUNT SAVED	SAVINGS BALANCE	STILL NEED TO SAVE....

NOTES

_____

_____

_____

_____

_____

SAVINGS Goal Tracker

Saving for: _____   Amount needed: _____   Due date: _____

DATE	AMOUNT SAVED	SAVINGS BALANCE	STILL NEED TO SAVE....

NOTES

_____

_____

_____

_____

SAVINGS Goal Tracker

Saving for: _____   Amount needed: _____   Due date: _____

DATE	AMOUNT SAVED	SAVINGS BALANCE	STILL NEED TO SAVE....

NOTES

_____

_____

_____

_____

SAVINGS Goal Tracker

Saving for: _____   Amount needed: _____   Due date: _____

DATE	AMOUNT SAVED	SAVINGS BALANCE	STILL NEED TO SAVE....

NOTES

_____

_____

_____

_____

SAVINGS Goal Tracker

Saving for: _____   Amount needed: _____   Due date: _____

DATE	AMOUNT SAVED	SAVINGS BALANCE	STILL NEED TO SAVE....

NOTES

_____

_____

_____

_____

SAVINGS Goal Tracker

Saving for: _____   Amount needed: _____   Due date: _____

DATE	AMOUNT SAVED	SAVINGS BALANCE	STILL NEED TO SAVE....

NOTES

_____

_____

_____

_____

_____

SAVINGS Goal Tracker

Saving for: _____   Amount needed: _____   Due date: _____

DATE	AMOUNT SAVED	SAVINGS BALANCE	STILL NEED TO SAVE....

NOTES

_____

_____

_____

_____

SAVINGS Goal Tracker

Saving for: _____   Amount needed: _____   Due date: _____

DATE	AMOUNT SAVED	SAVINGS BALANCE	STILL NEED TO SAVE....

NOTES

_____

_____

_____

_____

SAVINGS Goal Tracker

Saving for: _____   Amount needed: _____   Due date: _____

DATE	AMOUNT SAVED	SAVINGS BALANCE	STILL NEED TO SAVE....

NOTES

_____

_____

_____

_____

_____

SAVINGS Goal Tracker

Saving for: _____   Amount needed: _____   Due date: _____

DATE	AMOUNT SAVED	SAVINGS BALANCE	STILL NEED TO SAVE....

NOTES

_____

_____

_____

_____

SAVINGS Goal Tracker

Saving for: _____   Amount needed: _____   Due date: _____

DATE	AMOUNT SAVED	SAVINGS BALANCE	STILL NEED TO SAVE....

NOTES

_____

_____

_____

_____

SAVINGS Goal Tracker

Saving for: _____   Amount needed: _____   Due date: _____

DATE	AMOUNT SAVED	SAVINGS BALANCE	STILL NEED TO SAVE....

NOTES

_____

_____

_____

_____

SAVINGS Goal Tracker

Saving for: _____   Amount needed: _____   Due date: _____

DATE	AMOUNT SAVED	SAVINGS BALANCE	STILL NEED TO SAVE....

NOTES

_____

_____

_____

_____

SAVINGS Goal Tracker

Saving for: _____   Amount needed: _____   Due date: _____

DATE	AMOUNT SAVED	SAVINGS BALANCE	STILL NEED TO SAVE....

NOTES

_____

_____

_____

_____

SAVINGS Goal Tracker

Saving for: _____   Amount needed: _____   Due date: _____

DATE	AMOUNT SAVED	SAVINGS BALANCE	STILL NEED TO SAVE....

NOTES

_____

_____

_____

_____

SAVINGS Goal Tracker

Saving for: _____   Amount needed: _____   Due date: _____

DATE	AMOUNT SAVED	SAVINGS BALANCE	STILL NEED TO SAVE....

NOTES

_____

_____

_____

_____

SAVINGS Goal Tracker

Saving for: _____   Amount needed: _____   Due date: _____

DATE	AMOUNT SAVED	SAVINGS BALANCE	STILL NEED TO SAVE....

NOTES

_____

_____

_____

_____

SAVINGS Goal Tracker

Saving for: _____   Amount needed: _____   Due date: _____

DATE	AMOUNT SAVED	SAVINGS BALANCE	STILL NEED TO SAVE....

NOTES

_____

_____

_____

_____

SAVINGS Goal Tracker

Saving for: _____   Amount needed: _____   Due date: _____

DATE	AMOUNT SAVED	SAVINGS BALANCE	STILL NEED TO SAVE....

NOTES

_____

_____

_____

_____

SAVINGS Goal Tracker

Saving for: _____   Amount needed: _____   Due date: _____

DATE	AMOUNT SAVED	SAVINGS BALANCE	STILL NEED TO SAVE....

NOTES

_____

_____

_____

_____

SAVINGS Goal Tracker

Saving for: _____   Amount needed: _____   Due date: _____

DATE	AMOUNT SAVED	SAVINGS BALANCE	STILL NEED TO SAVE....

NOTES

_____

_____

_____

_____

SAVINGS Goal Tracker

Saving for: _____   Amount needed: _____   Due date: _____

DATE	AMOUNT SAVED	SAVINGS BALANCE	STILL NEED TO SAVE....

NOTES

_____

_____

_____

_____

SAVINGS Goal Tracker

Saving for: _____   Amount needed: _____   Due date: _____

DATE	AMOUNT SAVED	SAVINGS BALANCE	STILL NEED TO SAVE....

NOTES

_____

_____

_____

_____

SAVINGS Goal Tracker

Saving for: _____   Amount needed: _____   Due date: _____

DATE	AMOUNT SAVED	SAVINGS BALANCE	STILL NEED TO SAVE....

NOTES

_____

_____

_____

_____

SAVINGS Goal Tracker

Saving for: _____   Amount needed: _____   Due date: _____

DATE	AMOUNT SAVED	SAVINGS BALANCE	STILL NEED TO SAVE....

NOTES

_____

_____

_____

_____

SAVINGS Goal Tracker

Saving for: _____   Amount needed: _____   Due date: _____

DATE	AMOUNT SAVED	SAVINGS BALANCE	STILL NEED TO SAVE....

NOTES

_____

_____

_____

_____

SAVINGS Goal Tracker

Saving for: _____   Amount needed: _____   Due date: _____

DATE	AMOUNT SAVED	SAVINGS BALANCE	STILL NEED TO SAVE....

NOTES

_____
_____
_____
_____

SAVINGS Goal Tracker

Saving for: _____   Amount needed: _____   Due date: _____

DATE	AMOUNT SAVED	SAVINGS BALANCE	STILL NEED TO SAVE....

NOTES

_____

_____

_____

_____

SAVINGS Goal Tracker

Saving for: _____   Amount needed: _____   Due date: _____

DATE	AMOUNT SAVED	SAVINGS BALANCE	STILL NEED TO SAVE....

NOTES

_____

_____

_____

_____

SAVINGS Goal Tracker

Saving for: _____   Amount needed: _____   Due date: _____

DATE	AMOUNT SAVED	SAVINGS BALANCE	STILL NEED TO SAVE....

NOTES

_____

_____

_____

_____

SAVINGS Goal Tracker

Saving for: _____   Amount needed:_____   Due date:_____

DATE	AMOUNT SAVED	SAVINGS BALANCE	STILL NEED TO SAVE....

NOTES

_____

_____

_____

_____

SAVINGS Goal Tracker

Saving for: _____   Amount needed: _____   Due date: _____

DATE	AMOUNT SAVED	SAVINGS BALANCE	STILL NEED TO SAVE....

NOTES

_____

_____

_____

_____

SAVINGS Goal Tracker

Saving for: _____   Amount needed: _____   Due date: _____

DATE	AMOUNT SAVED	SAVINGS BALANCE	STILL NEED TO SAVE....

NOTES

_____

_____

_____

_____

SAVINGS Goal Tracker

Saving for: _____   Amount needed: _____   Due date: _____

DATE	AMOUNT SAVED	SAVINGS BALANCE	STILL NEED TO SAVE....

NOTES

_____

_____

_____

_____

SAVINGS Goal Tracker

Saving for: _____   Amount needed: _____   Due date: _____

DATE	AMOUNT SAVED	SAVINGS BALANCE	STILL NEED TO SAVE....

NOTES

_____

_____

_____

_____

SAVINGS Goal Tracker

Saving for: _____   Amount needed: _____   Due date: _____

DATE	AMOUNT SAVED	SAVINGS BALANCE	STILL NEED TO SAVE....

NOTES

_____

_____

_____

_____

SAVINGS Goal Tracker

Saving for: _____   Amount needed: _____   Due date: _____

DATE	AMOUNT SAVED	SAVINGS BALANCE	STILL NEED TO SAVE....

NOTES

_____

_____

_____

_____

SAVINGS Goal Tracker

Saving for: _____   Amount needed: _____   Due date: _____

DATE	AMOUNT SAVED	SAVINGS BALANCE	STILL NEED TO SAVE....

NOTES

_____

_____

_____

_____

SAVINGS Goal Tracker

Saving for: _____   Amount needed: _____   Due date: _____

DATE	AMOUNT SAVED	SAVINGS BALANCE	STILL NEED TO SAVE....

NOTES

_____

_____

_____

_____

SAVINGS Goal Tracker

Saving for: _____   Amount needed: _____   Due date: _____

DATE	AMOUNT SAVED	SAVINGS BALANCE	STILL NEED TO SAVE....

NOTES

_____

_____

_____

_____

SAVINGS Goal Tracker

Saving for: _____   Amount needed: _____   Due date: _____

DATE	AMOUNT SAVED	SAVINGS BALANCE	STILL NEED TO SAVE....

NOTES

_____

_____

_____

_____

_____

SAVINGS Goal Tracker

Saving for: _____   Amount needed: _____   Due date: _____

DATE	AMOUNT SAVED	SAVINGS BALANCE	STILL NEED TO SAVE....

NOTES

_____

_____

_____

_____

SAVINGS Goal Tracker

Saving for: _____   Amount needed: _____   Due date: _____

DATE	AMOUNT SAVED	SAVINGS BALANCE	STILL NEED TO SAVE....

NOTES

_____

_____

_____

_____

SAVINGS Goal Tracker

Saving for: _____ Amount needed: _____ Due date: _____

DATE	AMOUNT SAVED	SAVINGS BALANCE	STILL NEED TO SAVE....

NOTES

_____

_____

_____

_____

SAVINGS Goal Tracker

Saving for: _____   Amount needed: _____   Due date: _____

DATE	AMOUNT SAVED	SAVINGS BALANCE	STILL NEED TO SAVE....

NOTES

_____

_____

_____

_____

SAVINGS Goal Tracker

Saving for: _____   Amount needed: _____   Due date: _____

DATE	AMOUNT SAVED	SAVINGS BALANCE	STILL NEED TO SAVE....

NOTES

_____

_____

_____

_____

SAVINGS Goal Tracker

Saving for: _____   Amount needed: _____   Due date: _____

DATE	AMOUNT SAVED	SAVINGS BALANCE	STILL NEED TO SAVE....

NOTES

_____

_____

_____

_____

SAVINGS Goal Tracker

Saving for: _____   Amount needed: _____   Due date: _____

DATE	AMOUNT SAVED	SAVINGS BALANCE	STILL NEED TO SAVE....

NOTES

_____

_____

_____

_____

SAVINGS Goal Tracker

Saving for: _____   Amount needed: _____   Due date: _____

DATE	AMOUNT SAVED	SAVINGS BALANCE	STILL NEED TO SAVE....

NOTES

_____

_____

_____

_____

_____

SAVINGS Goal Tracker

Saving for: _____   Amount needed: _____   Due date: _____

DATE	AMOUNT SAVED	SAVINGS BALANCE	STILL NEED TO SAVE....

NOTES

_____

_____

_____

_____

SAVINGS Goal Tracker

Saving for: _____   Amount needed: _____   Due date: _____

DATE	AMOUNT SAVED	SAVINGS BALANCE	STILL NEED TO SAVE....

NOTES

_____

_____

_____

_____

SAVINGS Goal Tracker

Saving for: _____   Amount needed: _____   Due date: _____

DATE	AMOUNT SAVED	SAVINGS BALANCE	STILL NEED TO SAVE....

NOTES

_____

_____

_____

_____

SAVINGS Goal Tracker

Saving for: _____   Amount needed: _____   Due date: _____

DATE	AMOUNT SAVED	SAVINGS BALANCE	STILL NEED TO SAVE....

NOTES

_____

_____

_____

_____

SAVINGS Goal Tracker

Saving for: _____   Amount needed: _____   Due date: _____

DATE	AMOUNT SAVED	SAVINGS BALANCE	STILL NEED TO SAVE....

NOTES

_____
_____
_____
_____

SAVINGS Goal Tracker

Saving for: _____   Amount needed: _____   Due date: _____

DATE	AMOUNT SAVED	SAVINGS BALANCE	STILL NEED TO SAVE....

NOTES

_____

_____

_____

_____

SAVINGS Goal Tracker

Saving for: _____   Amount needed: _____   Due date: _____

DATE	AMOUNT SAVED	SAVINGS BALANCE	STILL NEED TO SAVE....

NOTES

_____

_____

_____

_____

SAVINGS Goal Tracker

Saving for: _____   Amount needed: _____   Due date: _____

DATE	AMOUNT SAVED	SAVINGS BALANCE	STILL NEED TO SAVE....

NOTES

_____

_____

_____

_____

SAVINGS Goal Tracker

Saving for: _____   Amount needed: _____   Due date: _____

DATE	AMOUNT SAVED	SAVINGS BALANCE	STILL NEED TO SAVE....

NOTES

_____

_____

_____

_____

SAVINGS Goal Tracker

Saving for: _____   Amount needed: _____   Due date: _____

DATE	AMOUNT SAVED	SAVINGS BALANCE	STILL NEED TO SAVE....

NOTES

_____

_____

_____

_____

SAVINGS Goal Tracker

Saving for: _____   Amount needed: _____   Due date: _____

DATE	AMOUNT SAVED	SAVINGS BALANCE	STILL NEED TO SAVE....

NOTES

_____

_____

_____

_____

SAVINGS Goal Tracker

Saving for: _____   Amount needed: _____   Due date: _____

DATE	AMOUNT SAVED	SAVINGS BALANCE	STILL NEED TO SAVE....

NOTES

_____

_____

_____

_____

SAVINGS Goal Tracker

Saving for: _____   Amount needed: _____   Due date: _____

DATE	AMOUNT SAVED	SAVINGS BALANCE	STILL NEED TO SAVE....

NOTES

_____

_____

_____

_____

SAVINGS Goal Tracker

Saving for: _____   Amount needed: _____   Due date: _____

DATE	AMOUNT SAVED	SAVINGS BALANCE	STILL NEED TO SAVE....

NOTES

_____

_____

_____

_____

SAVINGS Goal Tracker

Saving for: _____   Amount needed: _____   Due date: _____

DATE	AMOUNT SAVED	SAVINGS BALANCE	STILL NEED TO SAVE....

NOTES

_____

_____

_____

_____

SAVINGS Goal Tracker

Saving for: _____   Amount needed: _____   Due date: _____

DATE	AMOUNT SAVED	SAVINGS BALANCE	STILL NEED TO SAVE....

NOTES

_____

_____

_____

_____

SAVINGS Goal Tracker

Saving for: _____   Amount needed: _____   Due date: _____

DATE	AMOUNT SAVED	SAVINGS BALANCE	STILL NEED TO SAVE....

NOTES

_____

_____

_____

_____

SAVINGS Goal Tracker

Saving for: _____   Amount needed: _____   Due date: _____

DATE	AMOUNT SAVED	SAVINGS BALANCE	STILL NEED TO SAVE....

NOTES

_____

_____

_____

_____

_____

SAVINGS Goal Tracker

Saving for: _____   Amount needed: _____   Due date: _____

DATE	AMOUNT SAVED	SAVINGS BALANCE	STILL NEED TO SAVE....

NOTES

_____

_____

_____

_____

SAVINGS Goal Tracker

Saving for: _____   Amount needed: _____   Due date: _____

DATE	AMOUNT SAVED	SAVINGS BALANCE	STILL NEED TO SAVE....

NOTES

_____

_____

_____

_____

SAVINGS Goal Tracker

Saving for: _____   Amount needed: _____   Due date: _____

DATE	AMOUNT SAVED	SAVINGS BALANCE	STILL NEED TO SAVE....

NOTES

_____

_____

_____

_____

SAVINGS Goal Tracker

Saving for: _____   Amount needed:_____   Due date:_____

DATE	AMOUNT SAVED	SAVINGS BALANCE	STILL NEED TO SAVE....

NOTES

_____

_____

_____

_____

SAVINGS Goal Tracker

Saving for: _____   Amount needed: _____   Due date: _____

DATE	AMOUNT SAVED	SAVINGS BALANCE	STILL NEED TO SAVE....

NOTES

_____

_____

_____

_____

Takeaway notes:

_____

_____

_____

_____

_____

Year of use:

_____